ALONE
TOGETHER

Question, connect and take action to become better citizens
with a brighter future. Now that's smart thinking!

ALONE
TOGETHER

A CURIOUS EXPLORATION
OF LONELINESS

PETTI FONG

ILLUSTRATED BY
JONATHAN DYCK

ORCA BOOK PUBLISHERS

Published in Canada and the United States
in 2024 by Orca Book Publishers.
orcabook.com

Library and Archives Canada Cataloguing in Publication
Title: Alone together : a curious exploration of loneliness / Petti Fong ; illustrated by Jonathan Dyck.
Names: Fong, Petti, author. | Dyck, Jonathan, illustrator.
Series: Orca think ; 12.
Description: Series statement: Orca think ; 12 | Includes bibliographical references and index.
Identifiers: Canadiana (print) 20230218164 | Canadiana (ebook) 20230218172 |
ISBN 9781459837232 (hardcover) | ISBN 9781459837249 (PDF) | ISBN 9781459837256 (EPUB)
Subjects: LCSH: Loneliness in children—Juvenile literature. | LCSH: Loneliness—Juvenile literature.
Classification: LCC BF723.L64 F66 2024 | DDC j155.9/2—dc23

Library of Congress Control Number: 2023935826

Summary: This illustrated nonfiction book for middle-grade readers explores
loneliness and the lessons we can learn about connection even when we're alone.

Orca Book Publishers is committed to reducing the consumption of nonrenewable resources in the
production of our books. We make every effort to use materials that support a sustainable future.

Orca Book Publishers gratefully acknowledges the support for its publishing programs provided
by the following agencies: the Government of Canada, the Canada Council for the Arts and the
Province of British Columbia through the BC Arts Council and the Book Publishing Tax Credit.

Cover and interior artwork by Jonathan Dyck
Edited by Kirstie Hudson
Design by Troy Cunningham

Printed and bound in the South Korea.

27   26   25   24   •   1   2   3   4

For my family and for the listeners who went with us on the journey of finding out what we can learn from loneliness. And for anyone who ever thought they were alone in feeling lonely.

CONTENTS

Introduction 1
    Empty Classrooms 2
    It Starts with Curiosity 3

Chapter One: CHILD ALONE 5
    Orphans in Fiction 6
    Lost in the Story 7
    Spider-Man, Spider-Man 10
    Alone 10

Chapter Two: TAKING A STAND AGAINST LONELINESS 13
    Superheroes 13
    A Wild Ride 14
    Everyone Can Be a Superhero 16
    Longing for Belonging 17
    The Greensboro Four 18
    Civil Rights Movement 21

Chapter Three: THE WORLD AROUND US 25
    Bee-ginning with Bees 25
    Kind Words 27
    Trees Break, Trees Grow Together 29
    Nature Heals 31
    Want to Go for a Walk? 33
    Get Up and Go 35
    People Walker 39

Chapter Four: WITH MAC AND CHEESE, YOU'RE NEVER ALONE 41
    China Lily 42
    Science behind Cravings 43
    Bao 44
    Have You Ever Eaten at a Diner? 46
    Connecting through Isolation 48
    Comfy Clothes 51
    A Father's Suit 52
    Clothes for a Greater Cause 54
    Science behind the Clothes We Wear 55
    Stretchy Pants 56

Chapter Five: THE WORLD WITHIN US **59**

    FOMO 60

    Boredom Lab 62

    Conquering Boredom 63

    Plant a Garden 64

    Imagination 65

    Kindness Matters 67

    Be Nice, Feel Better 68

    Science of Kindness 69

    We Are Alone Together 70

Glossary **72**

Resources **74**

Acknowledgments **75**

Index **76**

GOLERO/GETTY IMAGES

INTRODUCTION

On March 12, 2020, scary news swept through classrooms in countries all over the globe.

Schools were shutting down. The ***World Health Organization*** declared a global ***pandemic***. Teachers began telling students they had to go home. Exams and assignments were canceled.

I was one of those teachers, and despite the fears and worries about a virus that was still largely unknown, there was another concern. Some of the students I was teaching in college and at a polytechnic university didn't want to leave. School was their community, and they didn't want to lose their connection to a place and the people who gave them purpose and a sense of belonging. The thought of schools closing was scarier for some students than the virus. Some of these students had traveled from other countries around the world, leaving behind families, friends and everything they knew, to attend school in Canada. Others were on their

In spring 2020, classrooms and schools around the world shut down because of COVID-19. The pandemic forced students and teachers to go online to continue their education.
MASKOT/GETTY IMAGES

own and *alone* because they didn't feel close to their family or people they'd known when they were younger.

As a teacher, I had to tell students to turn off the school computers, gather their books and belongings and leave the campus. One student told me his parents in India wanted him to come home so he wouldn't be alone during a scary time in the world. He didn't know how to tell them that there were no flights he could take. He was the first person in his family to get on a plane and the first member of his family to leave the town where he'd grown up. Another student was stressed at the closure because she needed the school's internet connection to be able to talk to her family in Malaysia, as she didn't have enough data on her phone.

EMPTY CLASSROOMS

As students left the campus, many stayed outside, unsure where to go and what to do next. No one talked to each other. For many of us, words that had once been just words in a dictionary became personal—*quarantine*, *isolation* and *social distancing*. They were words we heard from others, from newscasters and from public health officials. They were words that suddenly became very real and scary. People were told they needed to stay away from others in order to contain the virus. Like many other teachers around the world that day, I and my colleagues decided, without speaking about it beforehand, not to go home to our families until all the students were gone.

Shortly after that day, when I stood alone in that empty classroom, I decided to start a podcast. My goal was for students and anyone else listening to discover that even if we are alone, there are things we can learn about ourselves that will help us connect with others. We can feel *loneliness* even

if we are with our families at home or at school with others. Loneliness can happen at any time. Before a pandemic, after a pandemic, when we are in a classroom full of other people or when we are by ourselves. Being alone and being lonely are different things. We will use the terms *lonely* and *alone* often throughout this book, but it's important to recognize that they have different meanings for people. We may want to be alone at times, but when we are lonely, we often want to feel *un*lonely, and that means we want to make connections. Being curious about the world around us and what we can learn from loneliness gives us a way to connect with others.

IT STARTS WITH CURIOSITY

Curiosity leads us to explore, and when we explore, we are open to learning. Exploration makes us want to ask questions. Questions can lead to answers. Some people think that being lonely is something to be ashamed of or to hide. Or that if you're alone, it means nobody likes you. What I hope you discover from reading this book and hearing the stories of real people is that loneliness is not a mysterious, unknowable thing, even if it can seem very personal and private. Loneliness can be unraveled when we share what others have learned. We don't have a cure for it. But loneliness can be understood. There are things you'll learn in this book that may help you understand that everyone feels lonely at some time or another. Loneliness can help you understand other people better. It can lead you to know yourself better. It can help you learn what it means to be part of a community, even if you think you are a community of one.

Let's begin with curiosity and start exploring.

We may be alone, but we are alone together.

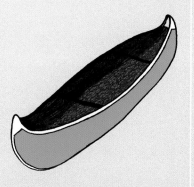

<u>one</u>

CHILD ALONE

Imagine waking up one morning to discover you are entirely alone. Everyone else in your home has disappeared. You look out the window. The streets are empty. There are no cars on the road. No bicycles. No skateboards or scooters. No footsteps. There are no planes flying overhead. Buses are not running. Shops are abandoned. Buildings are vacant. Schools are deserted. There's no phone reception. No internet connection. No electricity. No television. No radio. No mobile apps are working. It is silent and eerie.

Lonely.

It feels like you are alone on an island, trapped. There's no one else, and there's no way off. What will you do? If you're put in a situation where you have to rely on yourself, and the world outside is threatening, you will need to draw on your ingenuity and courage to survive. Maybe an animal, such as a dog, appears out of nowhere and becomes your trusted companion. The theme of abandoned children or children left

It can sometimes feel like you're alone or trapped on an island even when there are other people around.
JXFZSY/GETTY IMAGES

5

In movies and books, children are left on their own and must learn how to survive without adults around.

behind has been used in books, movies, television shows and even video games. There are many examples of the bravery and determination shown by kids when they're on their own, and the lessons they learn about loneliness when they're put in those situations.

ORPHANS IN FICTION

In the A Series of Unfortunate Events books, siblings Violet, Klaus and Sunny Baudelaire, who have been orphaned, have to overcome their scheming uncle Olaf, who wants to take over their family fortune. In the Pippi Longstocking series, a little red-haired girl with no mother and no father moves into her own home, where she lives with a monkey, a horse and a suitcase full of gold coins. Fortunately she is the strongest girl in the world. Author Astrid Lindgren once said of her famous literary creation: "Pippi represents my own childish longing for a person who has power but does not abuse it."

Daniela Contreras Pérez-Sosa, an expert on children's literature, says there's a simple reason why we like these stories. Young readers and adults too sometimes feel overwhelmed by what's happening around them. Reading stories about children

OLD ENOUGH

In Japan a kids' show called *Old Enough* has been popular for more than 30 years. It recently gained an international audience when old episodes aired on Netflix. Japanese culture generally encourages children to take responsibility at an early age and help their families around the house. In each episode of the show, children as young as two are asked to run errands for their parents. The kids are not really alone. There is a hidden film crew behind the scenes, following each child on their journey. Helpful neighbors are also informed so they can keep an eye on the kids.

The show's concept is to illustrate how kids learn to be independent and overcome their fears. One toddler who walks to the supermarket to pick up items talks quietly in a voice only he can hear (but that's picked up by the microphone) to keep himself company. The boy carries a flag so passing cars can spot him. Along his journey, which is more than half a mile (one kilometer), he gets distracted by a big stick, a police car and a vending machine that has toys inside. At the shop he remembers his mother's instructions to pick up curry, fish cakes and flowers for his grandmother's altar, but by the time he gets to the cash register, he forgets the curry. After leaving the store, he remembers and goes back inside to pick it up. The journey takes him 23 minutes.

In all the short episodes, the kids learn how to navigate various obstacles. The original Japanese title is *Hajimete no Otsukai* (which means *My First Errand*), and before the children are sent off, they're given a pep talk about how they're helping their parents. It's not easy for many of the kids. There are a lot of tears and sometimes outright refusal to begin or continue their task. But in the end, the kids show off the confidence gained by completing their errands. What seemed scary and impossible in the beginning ends with huge smiles, hugs and a new awareness of how a little courage can lead to big feelings of accomplishment.

provides an outlet for the helplessness they feel. Regardless of age, everyone at times has felt powerless and alone.

LOST IN THE STORY

Pérez-Sosa reads at least one children's book every day, a habit she developed when she was young. In all of them, she seeks inspiration and an understanding of what it's like to struggle. She believes there are lessons that everyone, regardless of our age, can learn from what children in fiction overcome when they're left on their own. As a grown-up, it's part of her job to

7

read children's books. She is a former instructor in Hispanic studies at the University of Kentucky and now specializes in teaching university students about children's literature.

Getting lost in a story helps her from thinking too much about her personal situation. For the last couple of years, Pérez-Sosa has been stranded, unable to visit her family in Venezuela. She knows it's not like the situations in children's books where kids are left on their own and have to survive in the wilderness. But to her the loneliness and isolation are very real. You don't need to be abandoned and living on your own to feel alone. Even kids who have food and shelter and families sometimes feel like they are on their own. Loneliness can be felt at any time and can leave a person feeling powerless.

FAR FROM HOME

Two of the most popular children's books of all time are *Lord of the Flies*, by William Golding, and *The Lion, the Witch and the Wardrobe*, by C.S. Lewis.

In *Lord of the Flies*, published in 1954, a group of boys survive a plane crash on an island. At first there appear to be only two survivors. But eventually others emerge from the crash, and the boys form a community. They quickly realize they have to work together to survive on the tropical island. Over time the boys gradually lose their humanity and descend into savagery and darkness. The island that is their new home seems idyllic in the beginning. But as fears spread that there is a serpent-like creature waiting to kill them, the boys turn on each other.

The Lion, the Witch and the Wardrobe, the most well-known book in the series The Chronicles of Narnia, tells the story of children who have been left to fend for themselves. In the novel, first published in 1950, siblings Peter, Susan, Edmund and Lucy Pevensie are sent to live in a large home in the English countryside. When Lucy, the youngest, goes off to explore her new home, she enters a world called Narnia by climbing into a wardrobe. There, in this magical world, the children learn about betrayal, courage and redemption.

"To be alone and to be a kid...we have all these perceptions that children are weak," says Pérez-Sosa. The reality is, there are lots of things children deal with and are exposed to. Surviving everyday life is often difficult for many kids. "We hear of so many cases of kids who have to face so many things: *depression*, bullying, questions about their own sexuality," she says. "Children have the capacity to process all of this, and we're surprised, but we shouldn't be. Children, not just in fiction, can handle a lot more than we realize." In books, and in real life, kids discover the strength that comes when they connect with others, and when they are on their own, they find out how to connect to their inner strength.

ON THEIR OWN

The stories Pérez-Sosa loves most are about kids finding ways to get off their imagined islands of solitude or away from real islands where they've had to learn to survive. There are books about children finding their way back to their parents after they've been separated and stories in which they've forged their own paths out of the wilderness, back to civilization and their waiting families.

Pérez-Sosa knows that feeling. She left Venezuela to go to school in the United States. But because of political upheaval in her home country, which led to the closure of some overseas Venezuelan government offices in 2019, followed by the pandemic, her passport expired. She couldn't get documents to travel, and the closure of borders stranded her far from her family. "Reading helps," she says. "When we read how children survive, it gives us strength to know it can be done."

Nikki Martyn is a big superhero fan. Here she is as a child, wearing her Wonder Woman costume.
NIKKI MARTYN

SPIDER-MAN, SPIDER-MAN

In the movie *Spider-Man: Into the Spider-Verse*, Brooklyn teenager Miles Morales turns into a superhero after being bitten by a radioactive spider on the subway. He meets Peter Parker and discovers he's not alone—there are others who share these special powers.

Nikki Martyn, the program head of Early Childhood Studies at the University of Guelph-Humber in Ontario, says the movie teaches important lessons about how to rely on people and fight through life's adversity to save ourselves and the world. In one scene, Parker tells Morales to get up and keep fighting. "No matter how many hits I take, I always find a way to come back," he says.

Martyn says that, like Morales, we all have an ability to connect with others even when we think we're alone. "We can't eliminate aloneness, but there's strength in being able to be alone," she says. "Loneliness is hard, but knowing that there are other people out there is important and can give us something to hold on to. We can all show kindness and consideration and recognize our uniqueness and our strengths." She says those are things we can always carry with us. That's resilience.

Children's book author Megan E. Freeman, pictured here with her family and friends, wrote *Alone*, a book about 12-year-old Maddie, who is left behind after her town is mysteriously abandoned.
MEGAN E. FREEMAN

ALONE

Children's author and poet Megan E. Freeman was in a book club with her then 12-year-old daughter when one of the young readers asked how kids as young as themselves could possibly live on their own. They lived in suburban Colorado and had just read a book about someone stranded on an island. They

were discussing how challenging it would be to survive in that situation.

Freeman started thinking about the loneliness someone would have to overcome in order to survive on their own in those circumstances. She went on to write a book based on that idea. *Alone* tells the story of 12-year-old Maddie, who wakes up to find that everyone in her town has disappeared. It's a survival story that explores the question, If you had to survive with no one but yourself to count on, could you?

"Finding food and fuel are extremely critical to your physical health and your endurance," said Freeman. "Your resilience in being alone is a different kind of challenge." For Maddie, the first order of business is figuring out what to eat, where to get drinkable water and where to sleep. But eventually she faces another struggle—how to deal with being on her own and the realization that no one is coming to rescue her.

In one section of the book, Maddie's loneliness is almost overwhelming. But the story doesn't end there. The last two parts of *Alone* are called "Acceptance" and "Reconciliation." Accepting being alone "is a huge step toward not having loneliness be painful or something we suffer from," Freeman said. When we can accept that we are alone and lonely at times, we do more than survive. We learn the lesson that we *can* be on our own.

two

TAKING A STAND AGAINST LONELINESS

Sometimes people are alone by choice. Other times they are forced to be isolated. Whether it's chosen or unwanted, solitude can create loneliness. But loneliness often inspires people to make changes in themselves and in others. Throughout history change has happened when people find meaning in their isolation and loneliness. Loneliness changes us, and sometimes it forces us to take a stand, to protest, to rise up or, in some cases, to sit down.

SUPERHEROES

Superheroes display extraordinary powers, abilities and moral strength. They have these qualities because they're not entirely human. Every superhero has an origin story that makes them mighty and, well, super. But the hero part of their story begins in a human way, when they are lonely. Their loneliness enables them to understand what it's like to

All superheroes have an origin story, and this story often starts from a place of feeling alone and isolated from everyone else around them. Superheroes turn that feeling into resolve to help others.
STÍGUR MÁR KARLSSON/HEIMSMYNDIR/ GETTY IMAGES

feel different from others. This is how their loneliness makes them stronger. Here are some of the things superheroes have saved us from:

ROMOLOTAVANI/GETTY IMAGES

MASS DESTRUCTION

ASTEROIDS AND ANNIHILATION

EVIL

CHARLES LEVY/WIKIMEDIA COMMONS/PUBLIC DOMAIN

TOKYO NATIONAL MUSEUM/WIKIMEDIA COMMONS/PUBLIC DOMAIN

GILNATURE/ GETTY IMAGES

MUTANT VIRUSES

A WILD RIDE

As a kid, comic-book fan Chris Doucher discovered that villains and superheroes have a lot in common. What differs is whether they use their powers for good or for evil.

CHRIS DOUCHER

Comic-book fan Chris Doucher is no superhero, but when a friend needed help during the COVID-19 pandemic, he was able to jump in. The friend was bored and lonely—she felt anxious and panicky, with a sense of helplessness about her current situation. Chris suggested she read a comic book about a character named Harley Quinn.

A few weeks later his friend returned and said she was hooked on the comic book. "As crappy as my day was, I know that now I can just jump into the life of Harley Quinn and not worry about anything else," she explained to Doucher. "That's pretty cool, and it's pretty powerful," Doucher told me in an interview.

Comic books changed Doucher's friend a little. It was a change Doucher understood. He'd been a lonely kid who often felt like he didn't understand the world around him. But that changed when his mother gave him two comic books. One was from DC, the other from Marvel—Superman and Spider-Man. Reading stories about those superheroes gave Chris an escape from his loneliness. It also taught him an important lesson about dealing with loneliness.

ALIKE AND ALONE

Doucher discovered that superheroes and the villains they fight have something in common. They're both lonely and often alone. The difference is that superheroes take on the role of helping others while villains are driven by revenge. What separates superheroes and villains is how they deal with adversity, says Nikki Martyn, whom you met in chapter 1. That's a lasting life lesson that can benefit anyone, from children to adults.

"Trauma, adversity, loss can sometimes create feelings of loneliness because you see the world differently than other people see it," Martyn says. When you experience the darker sides of life, such as losing your parents or someone else you love, you see things differently than someone who's never experienced them.

There are two paths we can take when something bad happens. "When we become resilient, we become a HERO," says Martyn. "We take on the role of helping and saving others." The alternative, which is the path often taken by VILLAINS, is dwelling on ourselves and blaming others for our problems. That's when we may become more negative and see only the cynical side of the world. When we think the world isn't supportive and caring, we want to hurt others in order to survive.

E. Paul Zehr learned martial arts as a kid to find out how to develop his superpower. He's written books about how ordinary humans can find their own superpowers.
E. PAUL ZEHR

Spending time on our own can help us better understand our own strengths.
FLASHPOP/GETTY IMAGES

EVERYONE CAN BE A SUPERHERO

Have you ever wanted to be a superhero? Or thought about what it might be like to exceed the limits of what others think you're capable of? Neuroscientist E. Paul Zehr teaches at the University of Victoria in British Columbia. He studies how biology, neuroscience and martial arts make superheroes. He first became interested in becoming a scientist after learning about martial arts as a child. And he learned about training his body to gain strength and power through reading comic books that his mom brought home from her weekly trips to the grocery store. Paul's mother loved reading comics, and she infused that same love in her son and got him thinking about how he could go beyond his physical limitations.

When he began learning martial arts at age 13, he started doing things he hadn't thought he could do, and he saw his teachers doing things with their hands, feet and bodies that he'd once thought only superheroes could do. Zehr says practicing martial arts, often alone, provided him with focus, determination and discipline—the same skills superheroes need.

"Think of the Fortress of Solitude," he says. "There's a feeling there of reflection and deep insight. The Batcave is similar. It's [for] a time of isolation." Zehr says superheroes take time to be by themselves, and it restores their strength and renews their faith in humanity.

BE A SUPERHERO—SPEND TIME ON YOUR OWN

It's important for ordinary humans and super-heroes to spend time alone. Being on our own is good for our brain health. That's when we do our thinking and figuring out how to go forward. We can only do the things we really

MASKS

When Nicole Smith of Woodstock, New Brunswick, learned that people needed masks, she wanted to do something to help. So, using a sewing machine she got for Christmas, Smith and her mother made dozens of masks for people to wear during the COVID-19 pandemic. "It's done so much for my family," she said. "It's given us a sense of purpose." Superhero masks were the most popular—Wonder Woman, Superman, Batman and Black Panther. Making them gave Smith a sense of having control over something that was overwhelming. It was a reminder that anyone can do something for somebody else. That's a superpower.

Nicole Smith and her mother sewed superhero-themed face masks during the COVID-19 pandemic. Making something that helped others made her feel like a superhero.

NICOLE SMITH

want to do and that matter to us if we spend time on our own thinking about what those things are. "The main lesson there is it's okay to be by yourself, it's okay to contemplate things," says Zehr. "It's okay to take time to think about stuff and okay to step back from things." He says you don't want to be ruminating all the time, but everyone, whether superhero or human, needs to spend time on their own.

LONGING FOR BELONGING

We all want to belong. It's a need that's existed for as long as humans have been around. It's not only a longing. Since our earliest history, being with others in a community was important and vital to our survival. It's easier to build shelters and hunt or gather food when you have others to help. Belonging to a community gives us protection against predators and forces that can harm us. When we're with others, we're part of a bigger story than the one we inhabit when we're on our own.

If you're ever tempted to do something you shouldn't— say, not wearing a helmet when riding your bike—an older brother or sister or your parents will tell you that you should or need to so you aren't hurt in an accident. Even that is an aspect of belonging.

Belonging to a group gives you access to knowledge, privileges and rights that others don't have. When you don't belong, divisions emerge. You are excluded. It is a lonely, isolating feeling.

THE GREENSBORO FOUR

Segregation is an extreme example of forced isolation. Sit-ins at lunch counters began in Greensboro, North Carolina. Four men walked into a "whites only" lunch counter at F.W. Woolworth Co. on February 1, 1960. The men were Jibreel Khazan (formerly known as Ezell Blair Jr.), Franklin McCain, Joseph McNeil and David Richmond. All four were college students who had decided it was time to change the status

quo. In a simple move that angered the white customers around them, Khazan, McCain, McNeil and Richmond sat down.

More than 60 years later, historian Will Harris, a scholar at the International Civil Rights Center and Museum in Greensboro, can sit at the same counter in Woolworth's where the four men sat. He says their decision to sit down that day changed American history. With peace and a hope for change in their hearts and minds, they walked into a deeply hostile environment. The simple act of sitting down there could have ended in arrests and jail time—and that was the scenario if they were lucky.

A segment of the F.W. Woolworth lunch counter can be seen at the National Museum of American History in Washington, DC.

RADIOFAN/WIKIMEDIA COMMONS/ CC BY-SA 3.0

In 1960, in Greensboro and in thousands of other places in the United States, Black people could shop in stores and order food, but they had to get takeout and eat elsewhere. They were excluded from sitting and dining with other customers who were white. The Lunch Counter Sit-Ins spread through college towns after the Greensboro Four took their stand to protest segregation. It was one of the most successful early protests in the *Civil Rights Movement.*

DIVISIONS CREATE LONELINESS

The lunch counter at F.W. Woolworth had something historian Will Harris calls a "limited togetherness." The ritual of dining together, among 50 or 60 people in one place, was a way of publicly being together. It created a sense of belonging. The problem was that belonging, at that time, had boundaries around it, says Harris. Blacks could order food there, but they couldn't sit at the lunch counter to eat with others, the white customers. "The people who thought they belonged were

The International Civil Rights Center and Museum describes the F.W. Woolworth counter sit-in as a "center-point of civil rights history and ideas—a site where time pivoted toward a more humane future."

TOP AND BOTTOM: STATE ARCHIVES OF NORTH CAROLINA/WIKIMEDIA COMMONS/ PUBLIC DOMAIN

The first sit-in was on February 1, 1960, and by February 4, hundreds of students had joined in.

present and could show up anytime they wanted," says Harris. "And not only show up, but in public they could carry on the intimate connecting activity of eating with each other."

It was a belonging that Black customers couldn't be part of until that day on February 1, 1960. The Greensboro Four asked for service and were refused. The police were called. The four stayed seated until the store closed, and then they left. A photograph of the four of them at the lunch counter was taken on the second day, when they came back again. Today Harris calls what they went through a historic loneliness. "One can imagine the sense of aloneness they had," he says.

OTHERS JOIN IN

On that second day more students joined the Greensboro Four. Five days later 300 students joined the protest, paralyzing the operations of the diner. At other lunch counters across the United States, there were more sit-ins. In some places there was violence. Students were dragged off stools, spit on or taken to prison. The students used their feelings of aloneness as the push to take a stand and make historic changes. The brave men and women in the Civil Rights Movement had known for a long time that their exclusion and the racism they encountered were wrong. They worked together to force a change that is still ongoing today.

TAKING A STAND BY SITTING DOWN

The bus boycott in Montgomery, AL, started in 1955 and lasted for 13 months. It began when Rosa Parks, a seamstress and activist, in a lonely act of defiance, refused to give up her bus seat to a white passenger. Her brave solitary act was the beginning of a movement that led to the end of legal segregation in the United States.

Rosa Parks was asked to stand up. When she politely declined, she was arrested and fined for being in violation of a city **ordinance**. It required Black passengers to sit in the back of the bus, and if white riders filled up the front of the bus, they could take over the seat of any sitting Black passenger.

Her arrest led to a bus boycott that lasted 381 days. For refusing to agree to a racist policy when she was told to, Parks helped spark the Civil Rights Movement. "I didn't have any special fear," Rosa Parks said. "It was more of a relief to know that I wasn't alone."

CIVIL RIGHTS MOVEMENT

It was a Sunday when the young man, in anticipation of going to jail, carried a backpack holding two books, an apple, an orange, and a toothbrush and some toothpaste. He looked down the road across the bridge. The day hadn't turned bloody...yet. But it would. It was March 7, 1965. John Lewis figured the Alabama River was about 100 feet (30 meters) below him.

Behind Lewis, who was just 25 years old at the time, were hundreds of protesters. They were on a march they hoped would give them the right to register to vote. The protesters were planning to make it to Montgomery, the state capital of Alabama, which was about 50 miles (80 kilometers) away from Selma.

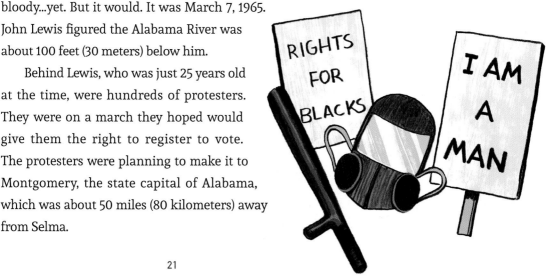

In 1965, civil-rights activist John Lewis led a group of protesters in Selma, AL, on a march to demand voting rights for Black people.

© 1965 SPIDER MARTIN

But something was blocking their path.

In front of the protesters were state troopers and police officers. They came toward the protesters after ordering them to leave and began knocking them to the ground.

In an interview 40 years later, Lewis recalled what happened. "You saw these men putting on their gas masks," he said. "They began beating us with their nightsticks, trampling us with horses, releasing tear gas. I was hit by a state trooper with a nightstick. My legs went from under me. I thought I saw death. I thought I was going to die."

YOU HAVE TO SPEAK UP

Even as he was being beaten by police on a day that became known as Selma's Bloody Sunday, John Lewis never fought back. He had learned not to through training he'd received while he was a student in Nashville in the era before the Civil Rights Movement. He said they were trained not to strike back if someone poured hot water or coffee down their backs and how not to respond if someone called them horrible names. "When you see something that is not right, not fair, not just, you have to speak up," said Lewis. "You have to say something—you have to do something." He was arrested more than 40 times between 1960 and 1966 for protesting racist laws in the southern United States.

REAL-LIFE COMIC-BOOK HEROES

In 2015, congressman John Lewis became a comic-book superhero. He wrote a trilogy of graphic novels called *March* with his aide Andrew Aydin and artist Nate Powell. Over the next three years Lewis went to San Diego's Comic-Con to recreate the march he did in 1965 in Alabama. Dressed the way he was at 25, in a trench coat and carrying a backpack, Lewis recreated his younger self in **cosplay** to show a new generation that you didn't need to have a costume or superpowers to be a hero, only faith and belief that anyone can stand up for what is right. Lewis said he was inspired by a comic book he read when he was 17 years old. It was published in 1957 and called *Martin Luther King and the Montgomery Story*. It cost 10 cents and told the story of the bus boycott and civil rights leader Martin Luther King, Jr., whose successful boycott led to laws being changed. "I read it and I reread it, and this book inspired me," Lewis said in an interview. "[Dr. King] became my hero, my inspiration, my leader. He inspired me to say no to segregation and racial discrimination."

three
THE WORLD AROUND US

Bees do it. Even trees do it. It's not falling in love. Yet it's just as biological, emotional and social. It's the act of coming together when we are at our most vulnerable. We see it repeated time and time again in different situations. When teams are down, they manage to rally and rebound. When nature destroys, it rebuilds even stronger. And when human beings are at their lowest points, they may find strength to overcome these challenges and that's often through connecting with other people. What can we learn from the natural world about working together?

BEE-GINNING WITH BEES

Let's bee...gin with bees. Ever wonder how swarms of honeybees are able to keep their clusters together? Engineering researchers at Harvard University studying *swarm intelligence* found the answer. Swarm intelligence is the study of collective

A Harvard University experiment explored the behavior of bees in a swarm when they're under attack. The experiment mimics what happens in nature.

CHRISTIAN NIEDERMEYER/GETTY IMAGES

behavior both in the natural world and in artificial intelligence. The researchers created an apparatus to see how a honeybee cluster behaves when it gets shaken up by the world around it.

They encouraged a swarm of bees to form a cluster on the underside of the device by attaching a queen bee and waiting for the worker bees to follow. The device moves from side to side and up and down, and its movement mimics wind and rain attacking a tree branch where a colony of bees has formed. The cluster is heavier and larger at the top, where more bees grip the branch—in this case, the underside of the apparatus. There are fewer bees at the lower end of the cluster. Apply enough shaking and stress to the cluster, and the bees at the bottom could begin to fall off. But bees have learned how to take an act of destruction and turn it into something else.

Imagine a cluster as a piece of pizza hanging off a tree, the tip of the triangle pointing down. The crust is the most stable part, and the cheese drips off the tip. In a hanging cluster, bees at the "tip" have fewer bees to hold on to. What the Harvard engineers found after shaking the clusters in

EMPATHY

LOVE

JOY

RESPECT

KINDNESS

WARMTH

CARE

the lab was that bees know when their hive is being threatened. And when it is, they do something remarkable without the queen bee having to issue an order.

Bees know that their best defense is staying together, and they do this by spreading apart and changing the shape of the hive to eliminate the vulnerable "tip." This increases the stability of the entire swarm. It also decreases the stress on the bees at the top of the cluster. When things are unstable and the whole hive is in trouble, instead of throwing off the weakest part of the swarm and leaving a few bees on their own, the collective takes action and saves the hive.

KIND WORDS

A few years ago, game developer Ziba Scott felt like his hive was under attack. Politics were dividing people in the United States. **Public discourse**—that is, the conversations people have about what's happening around them—was toxic. Civility had disappeared.

"We saw a real sort of terrifying public behavior, a lack of empathy and willingness and ability or effort to consider other people's lives," he said. "A lot of our communication systems are just so vulnerable to that. They just magnify and reward that kind of behavior."

The Harvard swarm experiment created a device designed to shake and rattle bees. Game developer Scott saw another apparatus that was causing chaos—social media. Social media is a human-formed system that can sometimes seem designed to shake and rattle users. On Twitter, for example, a user can write something to make others react with unkind thoughts or reactions. Those words can shake and rattle the system, and chaos spreads.

Sometimes I feel like crying and I don't know why.
— D

You and me both, friend.

Sometimes I never figure it out, and sometimes it just takes me a while to realize that something I thought I was ok with is actually bothering me a lot more than I thought it would.

I hope you feel better.

Send

Back

The game *Kind Words* connects people who need help or encouragement with other users who can anonymously send their support through letters.
LUIGI GUATIERI AND ZIBA SCOTT

Damaging, hurtful words and opinions spread quickly on social media. Hate is easily magnified and, in some cases, fueled by more hate from **trolls**. Scott wanted to put something else out there for the swarms of social media users. Instead of magnifying disruption and chaos and hatred, and letting hurtful tweets and posts multiply, he wondered if kind words would have the opposite effect. Could people talk to each other with civility and spread those feelings through **kindness**?

KIND THOUGHTS VERSUS HATE

Scott wanted to create a game that allowed people to feel they could express their thoughts without being attacked. The game would be for users who felt lonely, isolated and afraid to reach out on social media because they feared an unkind response. In the game they could find a safe place where players would get responses from other solitary users out there. The game is called *Kind Words*. There's no competition, no actual gaming and no interplay between different players.

A *Kind Words* gamer sends out a message requesting comfort, advice or even just acknowledgment. They may describe something in their life that bothers, scares or confuses them and ask for empathy, sympathy, recognition and perhaps advice on that subject. Topics range from relationship problems and family drama to general stress. The request is viewed by everyone, and replies come back.

On Reddit, one game user described *Kind Words* like this: "It's oddly soothing. People feeling unhappy or in need of advice write letters into the relative abyss, anonymously, and other anonymous users can respond. There is no back-and-forth—you can't reply to anyone who replies to you—so there's really no 'conversation,' just what the title says—kind words." Scott said the initial response from users was skepticism that this would work. "There's disbelief that we can have generally kind conversations," he said, "that you can put your feelings out there and you won't get hurt or eviscerated right away. But it works because of the community."

TREES BREAK, TREES GROW TOGETHER

Most of us are familiar with the word *isolation*, which means "separation," but have you ever heard of **inosculation**? It's a natural event whereby two trees unite and grow together. It happens when their outer bark is worn away by such things as rain, snow or ice or by their brushing against each other in the wind. When such forces strip away the trees' bark, the inner tissues are exposed. In response to the "wound," the trees self-graft and grow together.

When two trees have their branches broken and damaged due to wind and rain, their branches can join together to grow stronger.
MIHIR RANJAN/DREAMSTIME.COM

DID YOU KNOW?

The verb *inosculate* comes from the word *osculate*, which means "to kiss." Scientists use the word *osculate* to refer to what happens when one thing has contact with another. So *inosculate* combines *in* (into) and *osculate* (be in contact with).

Some species of trees are more likely to come together, and those are trees that are particularly vulnerable to the elements. It happens with trees that have thinner barks, like apple or pear or beech trees. The flimsier the bark, the higher the chance that the trees will inosculate. Once the trees join, they continue to grow together. Trees have figured out something that may help us humans. When we are weak, we need to lean on someone as we heal—or be the tree that others can lean on when they need to.

NATURE HEALS

Ever consider going into the forest with the trees to have a bath? Probably not! The technique is known as **shinrin-yoku**—*shinrin* is "forest," and *yoku* is "bathing." When we feel alone, sometimes the best way to reconnect with our bodies and our feelings is to spend time in nature. Simply put, forest bathing is good for your health. Go outside.

Yoshifumi Miyazaki is a forest-therapy scientist who works at the Center for Environment, Health and Field Services at the University of Chiba in Japan. He's written books about the effects and benefits of being in nature. Miyazaki says our bodies are meant to be with nature because humans have been separate from nature for only a fraction of human history. By his calculation, 99.9 percent of our time has been spent not in cities but in the natural environment.

Miyazaki says that being alone in nature resets our balance by reminding us that we are part of the world around us. That's why we feel the need to get back to nature at times when we're feeling anxious and lonely. Even the addition of a plant or a flower in a room can relieve stress.

SCIENCE BEHIND SHINRIN-YOKU

Your heart rate and blood pressure are lowered when you're walking in a forest. Stress hormones are reduced when you are surrounded by trees. Trees also emit an oil that can make your immune system stronger.

In one study in Japan, two groups of participants were given one-week vacations. One group spent the week in an

Being in nature has healing benefits and can make us feel less lonely.
PAMELAJOEMCFARLANE/GETTY IMAGES

urban area, and the other vacationed in the forest. The groups walked the same hours and distance every day. Those who vacationed in the forest had lower blood pressure, slower heart rates and better moods, and their immune systems were stronger than the other group's. The participants who'd spent the week in the city didn't show the same level of improvements in their overall health.

Another study compared a group of people asked to walk in an urban park to one asked to walk in the street. Their progress was tracked in the spring, fall and winter. The conclusion was the same—walking in a park is better for our health than walking in the street. "When we communicate with nature, we can break free of the stress of isolation," says Miyazaki.

TRILOKS/GETTY IMAGES

BRING NATURE TO YOU

What if you can't be in nature? We can't always go for walks in the forest, but there are things we can do to connect with nature. We can arrange flowers and have plants in our home. We can nurture a small garden or even a planted container on a balcony. We can choose to sit on wooden furniture instead of plastic chairs in our homes. For the lonely, being in nature can be soothing, and being around it, even in your own home with plants and other living things, will make you feel less lonely.

WANT TO GO FOR A WALK?

Have you ever moved away from a neighborhood to a different place where you knew no one? It's an experience most people face at some time in their lives. You have to learn new routines, figure out what's around you in your new environment, start classes in a new school and meet new people who may or may not become friends.

When Sandra Samuels-Allen moved from the big city of London to the smaller town of Rochester in England, she left the familiar and the comfortable. But she knew the change, as difficult as it was, was important because other things were missing in her life. She moved from one place to another in hopes of being closer to nature and finding ways to have deeper connections to people around her.

In the city, Samuels-Allen had focused only on work, but she hoped that by changing her surroundings, she could slow down her life. When she arrived in her new place, she found it hard not knowing anyone, and she couldn't figure out how to make friends. "I used to go out on my own, and I was a bit lonely," she said. She met people, but it was hard to follow up and make plans. For weeks her attempts to make connections and friends went nowhere. She recognized her acute loneliness and how much she wanted things to change.

Finally it was the night of December 30, and she was alone. Questions ran through her mind. "How can I help people who are probably in the same situation?" she asked herself. Loneliness

was not a problem only for her, she realized—others must feel it too. She just had to find a way to connect with all the other lonely people around her who were in their own homes, possibly thinking the same thing.

Samuels-Allen wondered if she could walk her way out of loneliness. She posted a simple offer on social media: *Want to go for a walk?* On her first walk, eight people took up her offer to join in. Now dozens of people join her group, Walking Workout with a Difference, for walks in nature. Being with others and surrounded by the natural world gives a sense of connection with the environment and people. Samuels-Allen made new friends, and those people made new friends. What she discovered was you can walk your way out of loneliness.

VOICES OF LONELINESS

Edvard Munch's most famous work began as a walk and ended with a scream. The painter was out with his friends in the Norwegian countryside. At one point his friends continued walking into the distance, but the painter stayed behind. Alone. That's when the landscape changed. "The sun went down. I felt a gust of melancholy. Suddenly the sky turned a bloody red," Munch wrote in his diary dated January 22, 1892.

Throughout most of Munch's life, he was often sick with respiratory illnesses. Today we might use the word *depression* to define one of his illnesses. Back in his time, Munch called what he was feeling **melancholy**.

In *The Scream*, nature comes to him. You probably recognize the painting of a person on a bridge with vivid colors around him, as if nature and his inner thoughts are threatening. The original title of the painting was actually *The Scream of Nature*. There are two versions of the painting. One is in the Munch Museum in Oslo, the other in Oslo's National Museum. Mai Britt Guleng is a curator and expert on Munch. Guleng said what Munch was doing was describing the scream from nature, a cry that could be heard within our ears, internally. "It was a symbolic representation of being alone in the world," she said.

GET UP AND GO

Nick Summerton is the medical expert for *Walk Magazine* and a public health doctor. He noticed a huge rise in isolation and loneliness after the COVID-19 pandemic began in 2020. Patients with long-term illnesses were forced to stay inside. But many people of all ages could still get out and walk during times of quarantines and self-isolation, even if it was just right outside their own homes. Family walks became more common during the pandemic.

Whether you are with friends or by yourself, spending time outdoors can improve your health and happiness.
RYANJLANE/GETTY IMAGES

DOGS NEED WALKS TOO

Going for a walk with your dog makes your dog's tail wag. But it benefits humans too. You don't need to have a dog to go for walks, but having a dog is a good thing, according to psychologist Stanley Coren, a world-renowned dog expert. When people are lonely, they often turn to their pets to give them a connection to another living being. He believes that dogs provide not just emotional support and companionship, but give all of us, adults and kids, a purpose and opportunity to do something for someone else.

Having a dog has the extra bonus of forcing you to go outside and do something physical. "A dog provides structure for you because you have to get up and feed it and that means you're not going to spend every day in bed until one o'clock," Coren says. "The dog needs to be walked and exercised, and that's going to get you out of the house and moving around." This could lead to meeting new people and making friends with others who are out walking with their dogs. Taking care of an animal who is part of your family gives you a sense of belonging and purpose.

There's science behind the health benefits of moving and having structure in your life. That's part of why dogs are good for us and why so many people during the COVID-19 pandemic rushed to adopt dogs from shelters. Some statistics show that one in five families adopted a new pet during the pandemic. Who's ready for a good walk?

Summerton is also a member of a British-based association called Ramblers. They're people who walk—or ramble, as they say in the UK—all over the country on outings. The association conducted a poll and found that one-third of the people surveyed said walking helps them unwind and improves the quality of their sleep. "If you get a good night's sleep, you often feel better and more engaged with life the following day," says Summerton. "The positive benefit of walking is it improves your ability to cope with the knocks and setbacks that life often throws at us."

Now, walking might just seem like moving our legs and observing what's around us. You might listen to music or have your ears tuned in to a podcast. Or you might be walking in silence. But research tells us that how and where you go makes a difference. Walking with a purpose, like

Sometimes wandering outside without a plan can be relaxing and stress-free, but at other times having a specific destination can give your day a sense of purpose.
NICK DAVID/GETTY IMAGES

going to school or the library or to visit friends or relatives, is better for you than just walking with no destination planned. Summerton says studies show that all walks are good for you, but if you have a place that you're heading to instead of just meandering or walking without a destination in mind, you'll walk faster and you'll walk better in term of health benefits.

It's good for you. Walking somewhere can actually heal you, not just make you feel less lonely. Make daily walks part of your routine, he says, and walk with others. When Ramblers groups get together, they not only walk but also take turns taking the lead. Leading others to new paths or places to walk helps build self-esteem. And building self-esteem can help people who are lonely, Summerton says.

PEOPLE WALKER

Chuck McCarthy was trying to figure out a way to make money when he was between acting jobs and needed to pay his bills. He'd noticed flyers everywhere in Los Angeles, offering various services. If dog walkers could make money by walking dogs, he thought, maybe he could earn some extra cash by walking people.

The more McCarthy thought about it, the more he thought his idea might work. He wouldn't need any supplies, and he wouldn't have to set up a storefront in order to find customers. He just needed fabric markers to write the name of his service on a T-shirt: "The People Walker." So what started as a joke became a business in 2016.

Some people were skeptical or found it hilarious and asked him questions like "Do you use a leash?" and "Do you also have to pick up people's poop?" But the most repeated question McCarthy was asked about his business was "Why? Why would someone pay to walk?" What he didn't realize, McCarthy said in a TED Talk, was that his plan to make a bit of extra cash by walking people struck a deep chord with strangers around the world.

He learned that everyone needs connection with others, even if it's just for a walk. It turned out people did want to walk with McCarthy. They wanted to walk with someone. McCarthy's motto, which has since spread to other places and encouraged hundreds of people, was Keep On Walking.

Some people thought Chuck McCarthy's idea of a people-walking business was silly, but it became a surprising success.
ROBYN BECK/GETTY IMAGES

CAVAN IMAGES/GETTY IMAGES

four

WITH MAC AND CHEESE, YOU'RE NEVER ALONE

RECIPE

Instructions

1. Boil water.
2. Stir in macaroni.
3. Cook until tender, 7–8 minutes.
4. Drain.
   *DO NOT RINSE.
5. Return to pan.

6. Add:
   margarine or butter
   milk
   cheese-sauce mix
7. Mix well.

If you recognize these seven steps, chances are you've reached for a certain blue and orange box in your kitchen at some point. And you likely craved its contents when you were feeling lonely. It's called comfort food, and for good reason. We want comfort food like soups, stews and congee when it's cold outside and we want to get warm. When it's too hot, we cool down with things like popsicles, icy lemonade or ice cream. We look up from our homework and need a snack—something gooey or sweet or salty and crunchy.

We eat when we're bored, and we eat when we're lonely. We reach for the food that provides us with what we need at that moment. When we are hungry for connection with other people and can't get it, we use the food that brings us comfort as a substitute.

COMFORT FOOD AROUND THE WORLD

- For Australians, it's sausage rolls and meat pies.
- The British love a bacon sandwich.
- My family in Panama cooks arroz con pollo—rice with chicken—at least once a week.
- It's cassoulet and French onion soup for the French.
- Tortillas and beans for Mexicans.
- Ramen for Japanese.
- Kimchi for Koreans.
- Spinach stew in parts of Africa.
- Couscous in Morocco.
- Rice and lentils in India.
- Congee and dumplings for the Chinese.

CHINA LILY

At Vilma Portillo and Cody Malbeuf's house in Prince George, British Columbia, a bottle of soy sauce made by a Canadian company in Ontario is the ultimate comfort food. When Malbeuf was growing up, China Lily was the only soy sauce anyone could get in northern BC. For him, having this brand of soy sauce brings back memories of his past and being around people he loved. When there was a shortage of the sauce in the winter of 2020 because of supply and delivery issues,

the beloved China Lily soy sauce was a much coveted item in remote communities in that part of the province. People paid five to ten times the normal price of $4 a bottle in order to get their supply. On eBay, one bottle was selling for $20.

"Comfort food is either a greasy, salty burger or China Lily. Just get a big bowl of rice, douse it in China Lily. It's the best," says Malbeuf.

He can gauge how bad a day he's had based on the amount of China Lily soy sauce he uses. When there was only one bottle left in the house, he measured it drop by drop. "Normally I'm a little more reserved with it, and then some days, I go all out. If it's a bad day, that's when I douse it," Malbeuf says.

Vilma Portillo and Cody Malbeuf always keep a jar of China Lily soy sauce in their cupboard for days when they want comfort food.

VILMA PORTILLO

Dr. Livia Tomova's research found that our brains react the same way when we crave contact with others as when we crave certain foods.

LIVIA TOMOVA

SCIENCE BEHIND CRAVINGS

Numerous studies show that loneliness triggers cravings in our brain for social interaction just as being hungry triggers cravings for food. Scientists first found this trigger in mice. Mice were isolated from others and then reintroduced to the mice in the lab. The neuron activity in the mice's brains was studied while they were apart and when they were brought back into a group. Scientists found a brain signal that was triggered whenever a mouse was in contact with others.

Livia Tomova researches how stress, loneliness and social isolation affect our brains. Not surprisingly, when people, like mice, are forced to be isolated from one another, they feel lonely and crave social interaction.

In her study, Tomova found that when we crave that contact with others, the neural spark that fires up in our brains is the same as the one for food cravings. And when

We find comfort when enjoying our favorite food or snacks, much like how we find comfort in the company of others.

JOSE LUIS PELAEZ INC/GETTY IMAGES

we're not with others, when we're apart and disconnected, our brains are hungry. "It highlights how important being connected with others is for humans," said Tomova. "One day of being alone makes our brains respond as if we've been fasting for the whole day."

BAO

In 2018 Pixar released a short film about a Chinese mother who loved to make dumplings. The name of the animated short was *Bao*, the Chinese word for dumplings. Baos are small, round pieces of dough stuffed with fillings. Dumplings are comfort food to many Asian people.

Bao was directed by Canadian animator, director and screenwriter Domee Shi and won an Oscar for best animated short. The film uses a bao to symbolize something more than a food that we eat. There are multiple layers of meaning. When we bite into a bao, we're never sure exactly what we can expect. The filling is hidden until it's revealed within the layers of dough. It could be sweet or salty. We don't know until we take that first bite.

MY DUMPLING

Bao also uses the dumpling to **anthropomorphize** an inanimate object. Anthropomorphizing means giving human characteristics to something that is not human. The dumpling is just a piece of food, but to the mother and the audience of the movie, it grows and smiles and reacts and changes just as a boy would as he grows older.

For many Asian viewers, the movie was not only about comfort food. It was a film about cultural and generational divides, and loss and loneliness. It tells the story of a lonely mother whose grown children have left home. She makes a bao, "raises" it and takes it with her everywhere. She protects her dumpling as if it were a child, and the dumpling becomes her son.

They share food together. The mother gives the dumpling a chocolate chip cookie, which he happily consumes. When he's upset, she gets him food from the fridge and puts it in his mouth. But as the dumpling grows up, he turns away from the food she hands him and goes to get his own food from the fridge. And as he gets older he yearns to break free from the comfort and smothering of the mother. She cooks him all the food he loved as a little dumpling, from noodles to braised beef, and makes a lavish meal for him of comfort food, prepared with love, in hopes that the dumpling will share the meal with her. But instead the bao rejects the meal and goes out with his friends, leaving the mother so dejected that she takes desperate action to keep her son with her at all times. The film shows that when we are lonely, we seek foods that remind us of times when we felt connected to others.

Dumplings are a favorite food of people around the world. Variations are found in South America, China, Japan, eastern Europe and India.

XIJIAN/GETTY IMAGES

Cooking meals together with friends and family can create lasting memories.

SOLSTOCK/GETTY IMAGES

OUR FAVORITE COMFORT FOOD

A poll of 2,000 Americans found that two out of every three people reverted to eating childhood food favorites during the pandemic. There was an increase in consumption of (in order of popularity) pizza, hamburgers, ice cream, french fries, mac and cheese, and spaghetti and meatballs. The poll also found that 41 percent of the people surveyed reached for comfort food to bring them happiness. And 85 percent of people said they gained weight while staying at home during the pandemic—the average was an extra 6 pounds (2.7 kilograms). Interestingly, 67 percent of respondents said that if they had to choose between giving up either their favorite food or social media for a year, they would rather stop using their apps. Comfort food does more than fuel our hunger— we need it to feel connected.

HAVE YOU EVER EATEN AT A DINER?

Diners are places to eat if you're in a hurry or just want a simple, quick meal rather than an elaborate multicourse meal. Traditionally these restaurants were designed like railway cars, and their popularity in American culture really took off after World War II.

Richard Gutman specializes in diners—he's curated museum exhibits and written books about them and even consulted on movies where diners are featured. He says diners sprang up in places where people working late shifts could get a hot meal that wasn't too expensive and eat quickly on their own at a counter before going back to work or home. The first diner was in a horse-pulled wagon in the 1870s,

The first diners in the United States were operated in horse-drawn wagons where people could grab a quick meal on the go—similar to today's street-food trucks.
FROM THE COLLECTIONS OF THE HENRY FORD

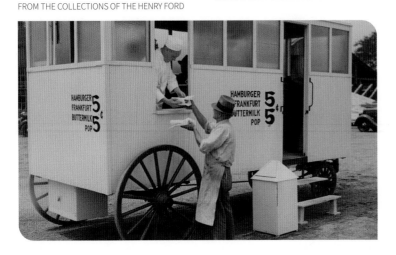

but today there are diners all over the world. Is there one in your neighborhood?

As an art student, John Baeder was first exposed to roadside diners as he traveled between Georgia and Alabama, and he developed a lifelong passion for painting them. He says they are unique places that anyone can go into and feel comfortable dining on their own. Baeder went to many diners over 50 years and always felt like they were places where you could be part of the community there at that time even if you were a stranger. There is a common lingo in this type of restaurant. If you go into a diner and you speak that language, you're automatically seen as one of their own and welcomed.

DINER LINGO

ADAM AND EVE ON A RAFT
... TWO POACHED EGGS ON TOP OF TOAST

A COWBOY WITH SPURS
... A WESTERN OMELET WITH FRENCH FRIES

FISHEYES
... A BOWL OF TAPIOCA

NERVOUS PUDDING
... JELLO

EVE WITH A LID
... APPLE PIE

COW PASTE
... BUTTER

BOWWOW
... HOT DOG

HOCKEY PUCK
... A WELL-DONE BURGER

CONNECTING THROUGH ISOLATION

Michael Tisserand was walking his dog, Scout, in March 2020—the early days of the COVID-19 pandemic—when he began thinking about diners. He noticed something. There were a lot of people inside their homes looking out. When Michael saw a cat looking out a window, the scene reminded him of the works of a famous American painter named Edward Hopper.

If he could have been around other people, Tisserand said he would have shared his observation at the coffee shop where he often went to write. But everything was closed down because of the pandemic. "There was a certain kind of light, and I thought, Wow, that looks like a Hopper painting," he said. "Then I looked around, and I feel like I'm in an Edward Hopper painting, and then I thought about it and realized, I bet a lot of us feel like Edward Hopper paintings right now."

Tisserand looked at Hopper's paintings online and tweeted his observation that all those lone figures in the art were reflecting what life was like during the pandemic. His one simple sentence was shared around the world, in Brazil, Taiwan, Canada and throughout Europe. It was retweeted more than 67,000 times and received more than 200,000 likes. His tweet said simply *We are all Edward Hopper paintings now.*

American artist Edward Hopper often painted ordinary people sitting by themselves in coffee shops and diners. Loneliness and solitude are regular themes in his art.

DES MOINES ART CENTER/WIKIMEDIA COMMONS/PUBLIC DOMAIN

He could have written *I feel like I'm in an Edward Hopper painting.* But he believes his comment was shared so widely because the word *we* resonated with people everywhere who were feeling alone and cut off due to quarantine rules—it allowed them to feel connected with others.

Nighthawks, Hopper's most famous painting, shows four people inside a quiet, late-night diner on an empty street corner.

WHAT OTHERS SAY ABOUT LONELINESS

Edward Hopper painted *Nighthawks* in 1942, after the United States had just entered World War II. It was a time of anxiety and uncertainty for everyone. In New York City, where Hopper lived, lights in public spaces were dimmed to reduce the possibility of air strikes. Hopper's painting shows three people sitting at a U-shaped counter in an otherwise empty diner on a dark street corner, late at night. They aren't talking. A lone clerk is behind the counter. A woman and a man are sitting next to each other but not interacting, and a third customer sits kitty-corner to them.

"Unconsciously, probably, I was painting the loneliness of a large city," Hopper recalled later. In another of his famous paintings, a woman sits alone in a theater, and from the perspective of the observer, the space is empty except for that one occupied seat. Another painting shows a man looking out his office window, high above the streets of a small town. Many of Edward Hopper's works depict people sitting in restaurants or at lunch counters without talking, hunched over a cup of coffee or staring blankly at nothing. "It's probably a reflection of my own, if I may say, loneliness. I don't know. It could be the whole human condition," said Hopper.

COMFY CLOTHES

When we are lonely, one way we find connection is through the clothes we wear. We wear clothes for ourselves. But when you think about it, the clothes we wear are statements and reflections of who we are. Are we casual? Or buttoned up? Do we like loose and relaxed clothes, or are the clothes we wear more fitted and rigid?

What we choose to wear reflects who we are.
CAROL YEPES/GETTY IMAGES

The message we are sending strangers who are dressed like us is this—we are connected. Have you ever encountered this? You're in a crowd of people you don't know, and suddenly you see someone wearing a similar style of shirt or shoes to yours. What does it feel like to see that? How we like to dress reflects who we are, and there's a good feeling when we know that someone else also has the same sense of style. We may dress like someone we admire— a real person or an actor from a movie or television show. This is another way our clothes connect us to people.

What could surprise you is that clothes may give another signal. Clothes are a physical reflection of our thoughts and desires. As we eat to fill a hunger, we dress to convey something about who we are and what we want others to know about us.

JJ Lee's book *The Measure of a Man: The Story of a Father, a Son, and a Suit* tells the story of what it was like for Lee to reconnect with his father through his old suit.

JJ LEE

A FATHER'S SUIT

When JJ Lee was receiving his degree from architecture school, he didn't go to his graduation. The reason? He didn't have a good suit he could wear. And when his father died, Lee felt ashamed about the way he dressed for his father's funeral. He wore a gray suit with a shirt he'd always hated. It was uncomfortable, but he didn't have anything else to wear. The lack of suitable clothing as a young man made him feel isolated and kept him from participating in things he'd wanted to be a part of.

One of the few items Lee received after the funeral was his father's suit. He kept it tucked away in his closet at home in New Westminster, British Columbia. The suit had his father's scent, Lee said, and whenever he saw it in his closet, it triggered memories of the man with whom he'd had a sometimes difficult relationship.

When Lee tried to wear the suit, he felt even lonelier—he missed his father and regretted not having more positive memories of him. So instead of remembering all the missed opportunities, he decided to create new memories for himself. Lee had his father's old suit altered to fit him, and his perspective started to shift. "My own interaction with the suit began to erase my father's presence within it," he said.

DRESSED UP

During the pandemic, Lee decided that after months of being isolated at home, he should go for a walk. It was April. The weather, while far from warm, was not cold enough to be an excuse to stay inside. And when he prepared to go out, Lee did something he hadn't done in a long time.

He got dressed up.

He wore pants that were a little bit tight. But they were nice pants, not sweats or well-worn jeans. He put on a tie and a sports jacket. He even folded and tucked a pocket square in the lapel of his jacket. He slipped on his loafers, picked up his fedora, wore his mask and ventured into the outside world. "The funny thing was, it coincided with someone else walking by," he said. "And he was wearing a sports coat too."

Since the start of the pandemic, when he'd started working from home, Lee had worn only casual clothes. "I was shocked that I wasn't the only person that decided that day to wear a

THE OFFICIAL UNIFORM OF SUNDAY

Sweatpants were invented in the 1920s by Emile Camuset. He founded the French sports equipment brand Le Coq Sportif, which has a rooster as a logo. The first pairs were gray and were called sweatpants because they—surprise—absorbed sweat. In the beginning only athletes wore them. Today everyone does. Sweatpants have been called the official uniform of Sunday. In one *Seinfeld* episode, Jerry tells George that wearing sweatpants is an indication that he's given up and "can't compete in normal society." Sweatpants have become a symbol. We wear them because we don't expect anyone to see us. We wear them when we are alone.

GEORGII BORONIN/GETTY IMAGES

sports jacket," he remembered. "I couldn't remember the last time I saw a person in the real world walking around in a tie." In that moment, on the street, Lee felt connected to a total stranger. They smiled at each other and nodded before continuing separately on their walk outside.

CLOTHES FOR A GREATER CAUSE

During World War I, when families and communities were torn apart, everyone was encouraged to support the war effort in whatever ways they could. Even though they were separated from loved ones, they found that focusing on a

During World Wars I and II, women took up labor-intensive jobs while men were away on the front lines. This changed the kind of clothing women could wear, favoring more practical items like pants and uniforms.

CENTRAL PRESS/GETTY IMAGES

greater cause gave them a sense of connection. People were urged to take clothes they already had and remake them. Dresses became shirts, and shirts from adults became clothes for children. You were supporting the war effort by reusing the clothes you already owned.

Families were told to stop eating lamb chops because lamb's wool was needed for the war effort. Women stopped wearing girdles and corsets because the steel used in them could be put to better use making weapons for war, according to advertisements in magazines at the time. Materials like leather and wool were needed for uniforms.

According to one scientific experiment, wearing a white lab coat can improve your test scores.
URBANCOW/GETTY IMAGES

With a war going on overseas in Europe, the people back home in Canada and the United States started dressing differently. Clothing became more relaxed and informal. There was less opportunity to get dressed up to go out for dinner or to socialize.

SCIENCE BEHIND THE CLOTHES WE WEAR

Did you know there's an area of scientific research called enclothed cognition? It's a phrase coined by Adam Galinsky, who teaches leadership and ethics at Columbia Business School.

The clothes we wear affect our psychological processes. In a series of experiments, some participants wore lab coats while others wore regular street clothes. Afterward they were given tests. The ones wearing lab coats performed better on the tests. In another experiment, all participants wore lab coats. But some

of the people were told the lab coat was a doctor's coat, while the other group was told it was a painter's coat. The participants who were told they were wearing doctors' lab coats did better in tests.

Do those results surprise you?

Here's one more experiment. Men and women had to enter a dressing room and try on either a one-piece swimsuit or a bulky sweater. The participants were asked to evaluate the fit as if they were considering buying that item of clothing.

The participants were then asked to do a math test. Women who'd tried on a swimsuit did worse on the math test then those who'd tried on the sweater. Among men there was no difference. The results show that the clothes we wear affect how we see ourselves and what we're capable of. Maybe when we're feeling lonely, we can change our outlook by changing our outfit.

Most people have a favorite sweater or cozy pants to wear around the house.

STRETCHY PANTS

We dress a certain way when we know we won't see anyone—like when we wear sweatpants. But have you ever gotten dressed up for an event or a party with people you like? Our clothes connect us to that social event. Alone and by ourselves, we dress differently.

Everyone has a favorite pair of pants or a T-shirt they wear when they're just hanging around the house. When we don't have to see other people, when we choose not to or when the choice is made for us—when we're studying at home, for example, or have to stay inside the house—what we wear changes.

Sometimes we dress to remember that we had a connection to someone or something from before. JJ Lee's suit, which had been worn by his father, was altered and tailored to fit Lee. When he did that, he felt more connected to the man he often didn't understand and who died before they could resolve their differences. The suit was worn by his father and then by Lee. It's now passed on to a new generation. When Lee's son graduated from high school during the pandemic, he wore his grandfather's suit, putting on a garment that had once fit his father and now fit him. We are what we wear. And we wear who we were and who we want to be. Connected.

Humans aren't the only ones who find clothes comfortable!
OS TARTAROUCHOS/GETTY IMAGES

five

THE WORLD WITHIN US

You might get a little bored with this chapter. And that would be a good thing. One of the most famous sculptures of all time was originally called *The Poet*, and the artist was Auguste Rodin. It shows a man deep in thought, sitting near the Gates of Hell. Later Rodin decided to rename his work *The Thinker* to reflect simply sitting and thinking.

People who see the sculpture interpret it in many different ways. Some see the man as being bored. If that's the case for you, you may be surprised to learn that being bored has a purpose, just as feeling lonely does. **Boredom** is stigmatized—that is, it's looked down upon in our society. The same with loneliness. Boredom is associated with things like immaturity or a lack of focus, because ours is a society that values energy and productivity. We don't like the idea that people—whether they're grown-ups or children—are sitting around being bored.

Think about it. There's a book called *The 7 Habits of Highly Effective People* that has sold 25 million copies. The book *The 7*

French artist Auguste Rodin created the sculpture *The Thinker*—a man sitting, lost in thought.

COURTESY NATIONAL GALLERY OF ART, WASHINGTON

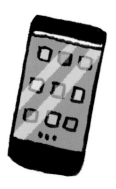

Habits of Highly Bored People has sold zero copies because it hasn't been published yet—no one has gotten around to writing it. The good thing is, there are scientists who study boredom. Learning what happens to our brains, emotions and reactions when we're bored may help us. If we can figure out how to use boredom in a positive way, we will learn a big lesson about how to be less lonely.

FOMO

Fear of missing out, or FOMO, is that unsettled feeling we get when we see others doing things that seem more exciting, more interesting, than what we're doing. Influencers on social media bring out our FOMO when they post pictures of themselves or other people living what we believe to be perfect lives. There is no FOMO when you see photos of people being bored.

Psychology professor Erin Westgate at the University of Florida in Gainesville began her career studying how we can enrich our lives and be happier. She wanted to find out if thinking happier thoughts can make us feel better and eliminate FOMO. Instead of envying other people's lives, we focus on thinking happier thoughts in our own head.

"Could we make people's lives better and happier by teaching them to use their mind to daydream and have pleasant thoughts?" she asked. "We all have moments when we're stuck in traffic or in a meeting or whatever where it'd be nice if you could watch television, but why would we need television when we have this nice great big brain in our heads?"

person19

126 likes
person19: #boredlife
view comments
goodvibes: So jealous!

SO BORING

Our brains actually have more information and memories stored inside them than all the Netflix shows available for streaming. But while it's easy to turn on Netflix, our brains aren't as able to quickly bring up good memories or happy thoughts. In Westgate's experiments, she started by bringing people into her lab to be alone with their thoughts. What she and her collaborators discovered was that the participants found it difficult to just sit and think—it was stressful for them, something they wanted to avoid. In fact, they were willing to do almost anything but be alone with their thoughts. Some said they would rather listen to terrible noises or even have electric shocks administered to their bodies.

Westgate realized that instead of asking study participants to be alone with their thoughts, she should really be focusing on understanding what it is about being alone with only our own thoughts that's so boring for many people. Rewind that even more. Instead of just our own thoughts, what makes *anything* boring? Why do we get bored, and what happens when we do? And how can we fix it?

Being alone with your thoughts doesn't have to be scary. Practicing mindful meditation can clear your mind of negative thoughts and reduce stress.
WITTHAYA PRASONGSIN/GETTY IMAGES

If we discover why we get bored, we can find ways to teach ourselves how to enjoy solitude.

KLAUS VEDFELT/GETTY IMAGES

If we understand how boredom works, then maybe we can go back and actually teach ourselves how to enjoy our own thoughts. That can go a long way in helping us enjoy our lives a little bit more, even when we are alone.

BOREDOM LAB

At the Danckert Lab at the University of Waterloo in Ontario, neuroscientist James Danckert and his team track boredom using different measures. One is a **functional MRI** machine that tracks brain activity and blood flow. "When we're bored, we see activation in the network known as the default mode network," says Danckert. "This is a group of brain areas that are typically activated when we don't have anything in the external world to do." The default mode network is activated when people are daydreaming or their minds are wandering, and it can lead to boredom.

One of the experiments researchers conducted tracked what happened in the brain when study participants read passages from two different books. One book was *Elements of the Nature and Properties of Soil*. The other book was *Harry Potter and the Goblet of Fire*. Unsurprisingly, people were more bored by reading about soil (no offense to all the **pedologists** out there).

WHAT'S IN A NAME?

Boredom has many synonyms (words that mean almost the same thing). *Sameness. Indifference. Apathy*. The word *boredom* as we understand it in today's terms is a relatively modern concept. It's been called *ennui* by the French, which comes from the Old French *enui*, which means "annoyance." Historically the words *lethargy* and *melancholy* have been used to describe a similar state of mind.

CALVIN AND HOBBES

Do you know Calvin and Hobbes? They were characters in a comic strip that started running in 1985 in 35 newspapers. A decade later, when the comic strip ended, it had millions of fans and was seen in 2,400 newspapers around the world. Here's how Calvin was described by his creator, Bill Watterson. "A rambunctious six-year-old with a rampant imagination," he said. "The kind of kid who wants plutonium for his birthday...a passion for excitement untempered by common sense. He's one tot that nobody wants to see grow up to be president."

Hobbes is a tiger and Calvin's roommate and best friend. He's somewhat naive but good-natured and is a snarky confidant. To everyone but Calvin, Hobbes is a stuffed toy. For Calvin, Hobbes is a buffer between the boring, mundane world of homework and vegetables, and a better place. The big world doesn't make him feel so small when he has a friend sleeping peacefully beside him. Hobbes is the friend who is real to Calvin, and he is the friend who helps him know that he is never alone. "Things are never quite as scary when you've got a best friend," Calvin says.

CONQUERING BOREDOM

What can we do if we are bored? Boredom reminds us that we have two competing sides inside us. Do we want to explore feeling restless and unsettled, or are we in our comfort zone and feel like there's nothing else we want to do or nowhere else we should be? If you're doing the same routine tasks over and over again—you wake up, you go to school, you go home, you eat dinner, you go to bed—you've settled for the comfortable. But if you're wanting to explore what else is out there, doing so will take you out of your comfort zone. When we're bored, experts like James Danckert and Erin Westgate say the best thing we can do is identify why we're bored.

We get bored when something doesn't have meaning for us, and that's why boredom can easily lead to feeling alone and lonely. It's on the same spectrum. The more lonely we are, the more bored we are, and the more bored we are, the lonelier we feel.

Boredom is an opportunity for us to learn what we don't like so we can challenge ourselves to experience new and different things.

CAROL YEPES/GETTY IMAGES

PLANT A GARDEN

The opposite of boredom is curiosity and engagement. We can engage and be curious about things and events and objects—it can be as simple as finding something that has always interested you and learning more about it. "We can't be bored and curious at the same time," says Danckert. "If you can cultivate curiosity for the world around you, you're not as likely to be bored as often."

If you find yard work boring, for example, switch to something else. Instead of just mowing the lawn, try planting a garden and growing something like flowers or herbs. Or if you are bored with raking the leaves, find ways to use them as a natural, environmentally friendly fertilizer. If reading is boring, look for different subjects that you may be more interested in learning about, or pick up a graphic novel instead of a fact book. You can also look for opportunities to read for someone else, such as younger kids at school, lonely seniors or people who can't read for themselves.

IMAGINATION

Curiosity can make us less lonely and bored. But there's something else inside all of us that also has the power to make us feel less alone. That power is our *imagination*. And it's not just for kids.

During the pandemic, Eliana Pauls, a four-year-old girl living in California, would take daily walks with her parents around their neighborhood. There wasn't much else they could do during the lockdown. Pauls couldn't go on playdates. She couldn't be with friends. Isolated from everyone but her immediate family, she quickly grew bored. But then she found something special—an imaginary best friend. Her name was Sapphire the Fairy. She wore different shades of blue and had a cat named Nova. Sapphire was always there to listen, and she was someone Pauls could share things with. Imagining her way out of loneliness worked for Pauls. Maybe you had an imaginary friend who did the same thing for you. It's more common than you may... imagine.

THE WOMAN WHO BECAME A FAIRY

As a child, Kelly Victoria Kenney loved wearing her Peter Pan costume. She was so attached to it, she barely took it off. When her mother made her wash the costume, Kelly would watch the washing machine and put her costume back on as soon as it was out of the dryer.

Kenney, who is now an adult, was a lonely kid. She didn't grow up with family members who thought like her and had her creative, imaginative mind. When she went to school, she imagined her stuffed animals at home would come alive and do things without her. "They were my little imaginary friends," she said. "I felt like a weirdo, and people made me feel like a weirdo because of my creativity."

She loved the idea of a boy who never grew up, the story of Peter Pan. All children have to grow up—all except Peter Pan. He didn't need to, but Kenney did. And being a grown-up brought a different kind of loneliness. Kenney got used to her loneliness as an adult, and at night, when she couldn't sleep, she would go for a walk by herself in her California neighborhood.

One night she saw something out of the corner of her eye. It was a sparkly twinkle on a tree. She got closer and saw that someone had made a small garden scene under a tree for others to enjoy during the COVID-19 pandemic. In the garden were painted rocks for a stream, little doors in colorful mushrooms that were

When four-year-old Eliana Pauls created her fairy garden on a sidewalk near her home to spread joy to strangers during the COVID-19 pandemic, she never imagined that a fairy named Sapphire would come to visit.
KELLY VICTORIA KENNEY

shelters for elves, and tiny tables and chairs for fairies to sit on. There was a poster by the garden, and it said:

Our 4-year-old girl made this to brighten your day
Please add to the magic, but don't take away
These days can be hard, but we're in this together
So enjoy our fairy garden and some nicer weather.

NOTES AND GIFTS

When Kenney saw the fairy garden, she forgot, for the first time in a long time, her loneliness. Her imagination took over. She knew she had one job to do. She would become Sapphire the Fairy for the little girl who had created the magic garden in her neighborhood. "Doing this every night gave me purpose in a horribly painful and lonely time," Kenney said. "I looked forward to my days again. I started ordering art supplies and little trinkets to leave her." During the first months of the pandemic, she left notes and gifts for Pauls.

In return Pauls made gifts and left notes and letters in the garden for Sapphire the Fairy to find. For nine months the girl and the fairy shared stories and even secrets. During this time, using their imaginations, Pauls and Kenney found a connection neither of them had had before. It made them feel less lonely.

Kelly Victoria Kenney saw Eliana's fairy garden and decided to become Sapphire the Fairy to inspire the young girl's imagination.

KELLY VICTORIA KENNEY

KINDNESS MATTERS

In doing something for someone else, Kelly Kenney, aka Sapphire the Fairy, kept the imagination of a little girl growing. It was an act of generosity that teaches us something

WHAT'S IN A NAME?

Imagine that a complete stranger randomly gives you $5 one day as you are walking down the street. You're told you have two options for what to do with the money: spend it on yourself, or give it to someone else by the end of the day. Which option would you choose? Now let's increase the amount. At the next corner, someone is giving out $20 with the same two choices. Which of the two options would you pick? Which of the two would make you happier? And does the amount matter?

A study conducted using this very scenario found that people who gave away the money felt happier than those who spent it on themselves, whether it was $5 or $20. Doing something for someone else—showing kindness—provided more satisfaction and happiness than doing something kind for themselves. It truly is better to give than to receive, and it goes a long way in helping us feel less lonely. Kindness matters.

about loneliness. Their story was later made public when Kenney shared photos of the garden. It went viral after a meeting was arranged between Pauls and Kenney, who dressed in a fairy costume. It was seen by hundreds of thousands of people, including Oprah Winfrey. "What a selfless act," she wrote. "Showed her magic still exists even in the hardest of times." Winfrey then offered Pauls, her parents and Kenney a trip to Disneyland. "[I] think y'all need to meet Tinkerbell," Winfrey wrote.

Kindness, like imagination and curiosity, can make us feel less bored and lonely. When Kenney first saw the fairy garden, she was feeling alone and isolated. But when she saw that she could help someone get over their loneliness, a change happened in the way she saw the world. Instead of feeling lonely, Kenney found a way she could help another person get over *their* feelings of being alone in the world. "There is goodness in the world, and we can all find some ways to help someone else," she said. She didn't realize at the time that the kindness she was showing to another person, a complete stranger, triggered a chain reaction that began inside her brain and ended up making her and other strangers around the world feel more connected and not as alone.

BE NICE, FEEL BETTER

We are expected to be nice to people we know and depend on, like our parents and teachers. But here's an interesting scientific fact: it's unexpected acts of kindness that will really make a difference in how connected we feel to others. Those encounters with people we don't know trigger the release of chemicals in our brains, which are sent from our brains to other parts of our body. We want to release those chemicals because they're **neurotransmitters**—they act like messengers inside our body. They're like DoorDash or UberEats, but instead of delivering food, neurotransmitters transmit messages between neurons or from neurons to muscles and other tissues in our body. When those neurotransmitters are activated, we feel good, we feel connected to other people, and we feel less lonely.

RON LEVINE/GETTY IMAGES

DOUGAL WATERS/GETTY IMAGES

SDI PRODUCTIONS/GETTY IMAGES

SCIENCE OF KINDNESS

Have you heard of a hormone called *oxytocin*? Some people call it the cuddle hormone. Another hormone called *noradrenaline* makes you fight or take flight, but when oxytocin is activated, it encourages us to tend and befriend—that is, reach out to people and want to connect. When oxytocin is released, it makes us feel less anxious and fearful, and the reward is we want to be close to other people. It feels good to have oxytocin released in our system, and studies show it can be triggered by something as simple as saying hello to a stranger or doing something kind for someone. Experts say the simple act of saying hello can reduce our feelings of loneliness.

"Whether it's a touch, a hug or just a friendly greeting of 'Hello,' it's very useful," says Paul Zak at Claremont Graduate University in California. He researches how oxytocin elevates empathy and kindness among strangers. "As social creatures, we need to be around humans, and if we're not, there's extensive literature showing that loneliness is literally a killer," he says. "It'll shorten your life as effectively as smoking cigarettes will."

Showing kindness to people releases oxytocin in our brains, which makes us feel good.

MACHINEHEADZ/GETTY IMAGES

CARING FOR STRANGERS MAKES US HUMAN

Oxytocin is related to kindness and trust. Think about it. We can't live around people unless we think we can trust them. Even if they're people we don't know. "It's a very unusual human behavior that we will care for strangers even when no one is looking," says Zak. He has earned the nickname Dr. Love for his belief that kindness is needed everywhere, from business boardrooms to playgrounds to school classrooms. It goes back to those random acts of kindness. Studies show that when lonely people are kind to others, even strangers, it lessens their feelings of loneliness. And the benefits are not just feeling less lonely. Showing kindness to others makes our bodies function better. Research shows that being a giver of kindness increases the body's ability to fight off viruses and reduces inflammation.

WE ARE ALONE TOGETHER

We are more connected than ever. Think about it. We have the capability through social media and our phones to reach anyone almost anywhere in the world. At no other time in human history have we been so connected to each other through technology. Yet these are lonely times for many of us. We often feel disconnected—from others, our surroundings and even ourselves.

Over the last couple of years I've interviewed hundreds of people—experts, scientists, historians, authors, painters, comic-book artists, video-game developers and community

RON LEVINE/GETTY IMAGES

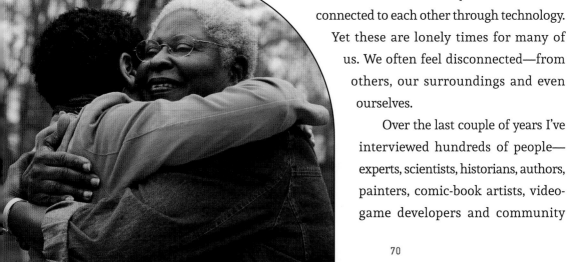

builders, and I've asked a lot of questions about loneliness. But the one question I've never asked anyone is, Are you lonely? I assumed that what people had to say about loneliness was more important than the question.

The fact is, we are all lonely at times. And there's nothing wrong with being lonely. We all have something to learn by being curious and exploring what loneliness can teach us. I hope this journey you've taken with me helped you understand that we all have something to give others, even when we are lonely. Sharing what we know makes us feel less alone.

Connecting with others, even over the phone, is the best way to feel less alone.
FAJRUL ISLAM/GETTY IMAGES

Are we alone in our loneliness? The answer is no. We may be alone, but we are alone together.

GLOSSARY

alone—separated from others; similar words are *solitary*, *solo* and *isolated*

anthropomorphize—give human personality or form to something that is not human, like an animal, a material object or a plant

boredom—the state of feeling weary and restless through lack of interest in your surroundings or due to repetitive events that feel dull and tedious

Civil Rights Movement—a series of organized activities in the United States in the 1950s and 1960s that worked toward achieving racial equality for Black Americans and eliminating segregation

cosplay—the activity of dressing up realistically as a character from a work of fiction

curiosity—the desire to know, learn and question, in order to reach a better understanding and knowledge of something

depression—the state of feeling sad, lonely or despairing, usually accompanied by inactivity, social withdrawal and reduced vitality

functional MRI—a procedure that uses a type of scanner known as a functional magnetic resonance imaging machine to measure and map activity in the brain, tracking where blood flows

imagination—the act of forming mental images of something that is not present to the senses, creating something in your mind that others aren't able to see

inosculation—to come together or join

isolation—the condition of being apart from other human beings or cut off from those you would typically be expected to associate with. In a health-situation definition, it means being separated from others due to contagious or infectious diseases.

kindness—the act of being sympathetic, helpful, considerate or thoughtful

loneliness—the state of feeling sad or dejected as a result of being isolated from other people

neurotransmitters—chemical substances that send messages to our muscles, nerves or glands

ordinance—a law enacted by a city

oxytocin—a hormone, sometimes called the *cuddle hormone*, that is associated with social bonding and is released when we feel connected to other people

pandemic—an outbreak of a disease that occurs over a large geographic area, such as throughout an entire country, continent or the whole world, and affects a significant portion of the population

pedologists—scientists who study soil and how it is formed

public discourse—the conversations around us; the public exchange of ideas and thoughts

quarantine—a period of strict isolation to prevent the spread of an infectious disease

segregation—the separation or isolation of a particular group by enforced separate housing, education facilities and services

shinrin-yoku—forest bathing, a concept from Japan that involves spending time in nature, surrounded by trees, in order to feel better connected to your environment and other people

social distancing—the practice of maintaining a safe or appropriate physical distance from other people in order to prevent the spread of a contagious illness. During the COVID-19 pandemic, people were advised to stay about six feet (two meters) from others.

swarm intelligence—the collective behavior of a group of animals, particularly social insects, like bees, ants or termites, whereby they appear to follow basic rules of action that they all know. The term also refers to an artificial-intelligence approach to solving problems using algorithms that are based on previously known behaviors.

trolls—people who post unsolicited comments online to intentionally provoke hostility, start arguments or attack others

World Health Organization—an organization founded in 1948 by the United Nations that connects nations, partners and people to promote a higher level of global public health, especially among vulnerable people

RESOURCES

PRINT

Burkhart, Jessica. *Life Inside My Mind*. Simon & Schuster Books for Young Readers, 2018.

Daniels, Natasha. *Social Skills Activities for Kids: 50 Fun Exercises for Making Friends, Talking and Listening, and Understanding Social Rules*. Rockridge Press, 2019.

Freeman, Megan E. *Alone*. Aladdin, 2022.

Jain, Renee, and Dr. Shefali Tsabary. *Superpowered: Transform Anxiety into Courage, Confidence, and Resilience*. Random House Books for Young Readers, 2020.

Kennedy-Moore, Dr. Eileen, and Christine McLaughlin. *Growing Friendships: A Kids' Guide to Making and Keeping Friends*. Aladdin/Beyond Words, 2017.

Sedley, Ben. *Stuff That Sucks: A Teen's Guide to Accepting What You Can't Change and Committing to What You Can*. New Harbinger Publications, 2017.

ONLINE

Apostrophe Podcasts, *Alone Together*: apostrophepodcasts.ca/alonetogether

"Children's taking action around mental health during the Covid19 pandemic," YouTube video by the United Nations: violenceagainstchildren.un.org/content/children-and-mental-health-videos

Civil and Human Rights Museum lunch counter sit-in exhibit: civilandhumanrights.org/exhibit/lunch-counter/

Kids Help Phone: kidshelpphone.ca

Kidzworld, a safe social network for kids and teens: kidzworld.com

Student Mental Health Toolkit: studentmentalhealthtoolkit.com

Voices of Youth: voicesofyouth.org

ACKNOWLEDGMENTS

I would like to thank my students at Langara College and at Kwantlen Polytechnic University. Their pursuit of their dreams gives me hope and confidence that all will be well in their future and mine.

To my family—Mom and Dad, Anne, Chet, Art, Sy, Austin, Andrew: Your love and belief in me as a writer have shaped my life. A special thank-you to Guillermo Serrano for being there from the first blank page to the last word.

To the Apostrophe Podcast team—Terry O'Reilly, Debbie O'Reilly, Callie O'Reilly, Geoff Devine and Allison Pinches: Your tireless hard work helped create 50+ episodes heard by more than 100,000 listeners in every corner of the globe. It has been a privilege to work on *Alone Together* with you. Thank you to the listeners who joined us on this journey. We may have been alone, but we were alone together during those times.

To the authors, academics, historians, artists, researchers, experts and everyone from fairies to game developers to hermit-crab breeders who graciously took the time to talk to me about the connections we can find in loneliness. Your words and insights made the podcast and this book possible.

Thank you to Kirstie Hudson, editor at Orca, designer Troy Cunningham, illustrator Jonathan Dyck, copyeditor Vivian Sinclair and editorial assistant Georgia Bradburne. Thank you Carolyn Forde, my agent. And I wish to thank my colleagues and fellow editors, writers, reporters and teachers for their support and friendship.

I teach and work and write on the unceded, ancestral territories of the Musqueam, Squamish and Tsleil-Waututh Nations. I am able to be present here because I follow in the footsteps of the immigrants and ancestors who preceded me. I honor and acknowledge the lonely sacrifices that have been made in the past which allow me to be here, now, and never alone.

INDEX

*Page numbers in **bold** indicate an image caption.*

activism, 18–21
   civil rights, 18–23
   helping others, 33–34, 65,
      66–68, 70–71
alone
   by choice, 13, 16–17, 61–62
   defined, 3, 72
   and isolation, 2, 8, 13,
      32, 72
Alone (Freeman), 10–11
anthropomorphize, 44, 72
artwork, 34, 48–50, 59

Baeder, John, 47
Bao (short film), 44–45
bees, 25–27
belonging, 17–18, 19–20
boredom
   defined, 62, 72
   and eating, 42
   overcoming, 63–65
   public attitudes to, 59–60
brain research, 43–44, 60–62,
   68–70

Calvin and Hobbes
   (Watterson), 63
cell phones, 2, 70, **71**
children
   being alone, 5–7, 10–11
   imagination of, 63, 65–67
   in literature, 5–11
   and positive messages,
      27–29
Civil Rights Movement
   defined, 72
   Greensboro Four, 18–21

Civil Rights Movement
   (*continued*)
   Rosa Parks, 21
   Selma march, 21–22
   voting rights, 21–23
clothing
   comfortable, 51, 53, 56–57
   cosplay and costumes,
      23, 66, 72
   and family, 52, 57
   and self-esteem, 51,
      52–54, 55–56
   during wartime, 54–55
comfort food
   and culture, 42
   diners and coffee shops,
      18–19, 46–50
   dumplings, 44–45
   food cravings, 42, 43–44
comic books and graphic
   novels, 14–15, 23, 63
communication. *See* media
community connections
   acts of kindness, 66–70
   and belonging, 1, 17–18
   eating together, 18–19,
      46–50
   and food, 42, 43–44
   need for, 3, 70–71
   and walking, 33–39
Coren, Stanley, 36
cosplay and costumes, 23,
   66, 72
COVID-19 pandemic
   comfort foods, 42–43, 46
   compared to wartime, 50,
      54–55

COVID-19 pandemic
   (*continued*)
   a fairy garden, **66**, 67
   limits to travel, 8, 9
   and pets, 36
   and sense of purpose, 17,
      36, 37–38, 67–68
   social impacts, 1–3, 14–15,
      48–49, 65–67
   supply issues, 43
   and walking outdoors,
      35–36
cultural heritage, 42–45
curiosity, 3, 64, 72

Danckert, James, 63, 64
depression, 9, 72
diners and coffee shops,
   18–19, 46–50
dog walking, 36
Doucher, Chris, 14–15

empowerment
   of children, 5–7, 10–11
   Kind Words (game), 28–29
   real-life heroes, 23
   and solitude, 16–17
   superheroes, 13–17
environment
   nature, 32, 34, **35**, 37–38
   small town, 33–34

family connections
   and clothing, 52, 57
   and separation, 1–2, 8, 45
   traditional foods, 42, 44–45
   walking outdoors, 35

fear of missing out (FOMO), 60
food, comfort. *See* comfort
   food
Freeman, Megan E., 10–11
friendships, 1, 17–18, 39

Galinsky, Adam, 55
gardening, 32, 64–65
Golding, William, 8
Greensboro Four, 18–21
Guleng, Mai Britt, 34
Gutman, Richard, 46

Harris, Will, 19–20
health. *See also* mental
   health
   brain research, 43–44,
     60–62, 68–70
   martial arts, 16
   stress, 31–32, 43, 61
   walking outdoors, 35, 38
Hopper, Edward, 48–50
human behaviors
   acts of kindness, 10, 67–71
   study of, 68
   toxic, 27–29, 60

imaginary friend, 65, 66
imagination, 63, 65–67, 72
International Civil Rights
   Center and Museum,
   Greensboro (NC), 19, **20**
international students, 1, 2
isolation
   defined, 72
   forced, 2, 8, 13
   impact of, 43–44
   and segregation, 18–21, 73

Japan, children's show, 7

Kenney, Kelly Victoria,
   66–67, 68
Khazan, Jibreel, 18–21

kindness
   impact of, 10, 27–29
   and sense of purpose,
     67–68
   and well-being, 68–71
Kind Words (game), 28–29
King, Martin Luther, Jr., 23

Lee, JJ, 52–54, 57
Lewis, C.S., 8
Lewis, John, 21–23
life experiences
   adversity, 10, 15, 29, 33–34
   and superheroes, 13–14
Lindgren, Astrid, 6
*Lion, the Witch and the
   Wardrobe, The* (Lewis), 8
literature
   children's books, 5–11
   comic books and graphic
     novels, 14–15, 23, 63
   real-life heroes, 23
   superheroes, 10, 13–17
loneliness
   acceptance of, 11
   in art, 34, 50
   coping with, 10–11, 14–15
   defined, 3, 72
   feelings of, 2–3, 13, 14
   and food cravings, 42,
     43–44, 46
   and sense of purpose, 17,
     36, 37–38, 63, 67–68
Lord of the Flies (Golding), 8

mac-and-cheese recipe, 41, 42
Malbeuf, Cody, 42–43
March (Lewis and Aydin), 23
Martyn, Nikki, **9**, 10, 15
masks, 17
McCain, Franklin, 18–21
McCarthy, Chuck, 39
McNeil, Joseph, 18–21
Measure of a Man, The (Lee), **52**

media
   movies and films, 10,
     44–45
   Old Enough (tv show), 7
   social media, 27–29, 60,
     70–71
   superheroes, 10, 13–17
   video games, 27–29
meditation, **61**
mental health
   brain research, 43–44,
     60–62
   challenges, 9
   and COVID-19, 14–15
   and nature, 31–32
   and pets, 36
   and solitude, 16–17, 61–62
   and toxic behavior, 27–29
Miyazaki, Yoshifumi, 31–32
movies and films, 10, 44–45
Munch, Edvard, 34

nature
   gardening, 32, 64–65
   healing of trees, 29–30
   shinrin-yoku, 31–32
   swarm intelligence, 25–27
   walking in, 32, 34, **35**,
     37–38
Nighthawks (Hopper), 50

Old Enough (tv show), 7
oxytocin, 69–70, 73

pandemic, 1, 73. *See also*
   COVID-19 pandemic
Parks, Rosa, 21
Pauls, Eliana, 65–67, 68
People Walker, the, 39
Pérez-Sosa, Daniela
   Contreras, 6–9
pets, 36
Pippi Longstocking (book
   series), 6

Portillo, Vilma, 42–43
public attitudes
    changing, 18–21
    towards being bored, 59–60
public discourse
    defined, 73
    and toxic behavior,
        27–29, 60

quarantine, 2, 73

racism
    segregation, 18–21
    voting rights, 21–23
Ramblers, 37–38
resilience
    and adversity, 10–11
    and being alone, 13,
        16–17, 61–62
    and curiosity, 3, 64, 72
resources, 28–29, 74
Richmond, David, 18–21
Rodin, Auguste, 59

Samuels-Allen, Sandra, 33–34
school, and pandemic, 1–3, 9
Scott, Ziba, 27–29
Scream, The (Munch), 34

segregation, 18–21, 73
self-esteem
    building, 38, 68–69
    and clothing, 51, 52–54,
        55–56
Selma (AL), 21–22
Series of Unfortunate
    Events, A (book series), 6
Shi, Domee, 44–45
shinrin-yoku, 31–32, 73
smartphones, 2, 70, **71**
Smith, Nicole, 17
social distancing, 2, 73
social media
    and community, 70–71
    impacts, 27–29, 60
solitude, 5–7, 16–17, 61–62
soy sauce, 42–43
*Spider-Man: Into the Spider-
    Verse* (movie), 10
stress, 31–32, 43, 61
students
    activism, 18–21
    unable to return home, 1–2
Summerton, Nick, 35, 37–38
superheroes, 10, 13–17
swarm intelligence, 25–27, 73
sweatpants, 53, 56–57

technology
    access to, 2, 70, **71**
    artificial intelligence, 26
    and mental health,
        27–29, 60
Thinker, The (Rodin), 59
Tisserand, Michael, 48–49
Tomova, Livia, 43–44
trees, inosculation, 29–30, 72
trolls, 28, 73

video games, 27–29
voting rights, 21–23

walking outdoors, 33–39
Watterson, Bill, 63
Westgate, Erin, 60–61, 63
Winfrey, Oprah, 68
women, during wartime, 54–55
World Health Organization,
    1, 73
world wars, 50, 54–55

Zak, Paul, 69
Zehr, Dr. E. Paul, 16

Petti Fong is a journalist, educator and author. She was a staff reporter at the *Vancouver Sun*, the *Globe and Mail*, the *Toronto Star* and CBC and now writes for *The Economist*. Petti teaches journalism, ethics and business communications at Kwantlen University, Langara College and the University of British Columbia. During the pandemic she created and hosted a podcast with interviews from experts around the world on the topic of isolation and loneliness. The podcast, *Alone Together*, has been downloaded by hundreds of thousands of listeners and heard in more than 30 countries. Petti lives in Vancouver, British Columbia.

Jonathan Dyck is an illustrator, designer and cartoonist. Since graduating from design school he has worked with a range of clients across various applications, from editorial illustration in magazines and books to logo design and illustrations for coffee mugs, T-shirts and posters. Jonathan lives in Winnipeg, on Treaty 1 Territory and the homeland of the Métis Nation.

THE MORE YOU KNOW
THE MORE YOU GROW

GOOD FOOD, BAD WASTE
Let's Eat for the Planet
Erin Silver
Illustrated by Suharu Ogawa

BREAKING NEWS
WHY MEDIA MATTERS
RAINA DELISLE
Illustrated by Julie McLaughlin

OPEN SCIENCE
KNOWLEDGE FOR EVERYONE
MONIQUE POLAK
ILLUSTRATED BY CATHERINE CHAN

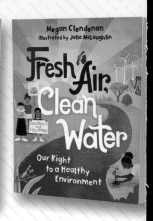

Megan Clendenan
illustrated by Julie McLaughlin
Fresh Air, Clean Water
Our Right to a Healthy Environment

Tanya Lloyd Kyi · Julia Kyi
BETTER CONNECTED
Illustrated by Vivian Rosas
How Girls Are Using Social Media for Good

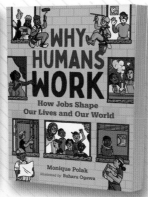

WHY HUMANS WORK
How Jobs Shape Our Lives and Our World
Monique Polak
Illustrated by Suharu Ogawa

SUPERPOWER?
The Wearable-Tech Revolution
ELAINE KACHALA
illustrated by BELLE WUTHRICH

GET OUT AND VOTE!
How You Can Shape the Future
Elizabeth MacLeod
illustrated by Emily Chu

SAVE NATURAL HABITATS!!

WHAT'S THE BIG IDEA?

The **Orca Think** series introduces us to the issues making headlines in the world today. It encourages us to question, connect and take action for a better future. With those tools we can all become better citizens. Now that's smart thinking!

PETITION

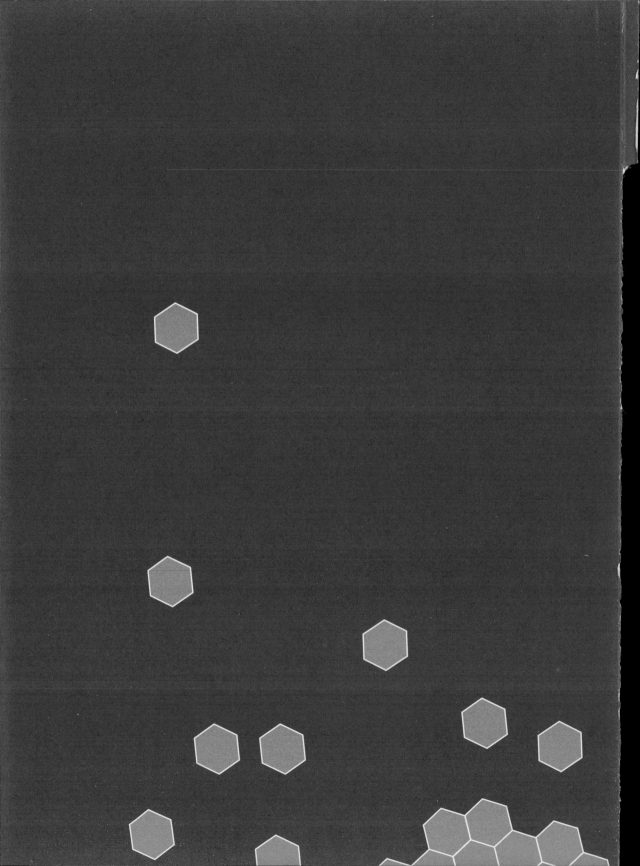